I graciously and humbly acknowledge THE ONE who opens the magnificent gateway and allows the creation of all that is. I acknowledge ALL IN ALL that is good, positive, loving, kind, compassionate, and peaceful. I acknowledge the truth and the light and all of those who are seekers of the truth and the light.

I acknowledge the genuine and joyful smile, which is the "kiss" of the heart. No matter how many times I fall, I acknowledge that this is a journey and I will become more seasoned with time.

—Atiya

Purposeful Dating

Manifesting the Love of Your Life
Through the Power of Courtship

Pub. 2014

PURPOSEFUL DATING

Published by Atiya's Light Publishing
A Division of Ingram & Atiya Enterprises, LLC
United States of America

All rights reserved
Copyright © 2013 by Atiya K.M.

All rights reserved. No part of this publication may be reproduced, distributed, or transmitted in any form or by any means, or stored in a database or retrieval system, without the prior written permission of the publisher.

Cover photo by Steve Butler

Atiya's Light Publishing
www.atiyaslight.com
info@atiyaslight.com

Library of Congress Control Number 2014904474
ISBN: 978-0-9916444-1-4

Printed in the United States of America

Dedicated to the ones looking to find the love of their life and willing to do things just a little bit differently to accomplish that goal!

Foreword

Having read the book, *Purposeful Dating*, by Atiya, allowed me the chance to look at how she and I met from a very different perspective. It also gave me a greater appreciation for the steps that we took as we began our own journey together. I met Atiya during a major turning point in my life. From a business standpoint, I was nominated for a national award in the United Kingdom, and determined to make a real difference in the lives of young people through BaylorIC Worldwide. As its founder, my mission was to create champions on and off the field using the sport of cricket as a vehicle. From a personal position, I had reached the conclusion that it was time for me to get married and connect with someone who had depth and was rooted in spirituality and principled living.

During that time, Atiya had just released her book, *From Ordinary to Extraordinary*, and was providing life and purpose coaching. I sent her some of my work and requested feedback. Needless to say I won the Community Champion Award for significant contributions in the community using sports and I also won the girl.

Initially when Atiya asked me to write the foreword, I could not imagine what of value I could add to a book about dating and courtship. It wasn't until I actually read her book that I realized what she outlined in *Purposeful Dating* is the exact process she and I went through prior to getting married. As the relationship progressed, we grew to a healthy respect for one another because neither one of us were willing to compromise ourselves, our integrity, our passion, and our purpose. We were very clear about what we wanted in our lives and were willing to walk away from it if it did not fit. We asked the tough questions and made no apologies for it. We both wanted a successful, loving, and healthy marriage and were determined to create an enduring relationship. However, we knew that in order to do so, we had to lay a strong foundation which started out by being honest with ourselves and each other.

Atiya is the founder of The Marriage Tree. She has, over the past 25-years, dedicated her life to honing her craft and indeed, her calling – to empower, build and maximize human potential by affecting profound transformation in people's attitudes, perspectives and behaviors. She has been the catalyst responsible for inspiring countless people worldwide to realize their dreams and achieve joy, success and fulfilment in life. Now she's bringing all her past experiences, education, and business development skills from her considerable history as a speaker, author, and life and purpose coach to focus on her core message: marital harmony ~ extended and profound.

In the book, she provides a step-by-step guide of what to do from the very thought of meeting someone right through to saying, "I do." The questions outlined in the book, which are representative of the type of questions we asked when we walked through the process, will help you to discover your own truth and set the tone for receiving Mr. or Mrs. Right into your life.

But this isn't just a book about the steps to take when you have decided you are ready to get married. Given the divorce rates and the overwhelming number of people not getting married, the self-development and marriage preparation components offered in this book is of tremendous value helping the reader to get it right the first time. It also greatly reduces the risk of making an incompatible choice. Atiya states, "Discovering and accepting your own truth is done prior to making a connection with someone else. To prepare for marriage and connect with the one person who is compatible to you, it is important to know who you are and accept the beautiful gift that you are."

Few couples ask foundational questions that go to the heart of the matter. However, even fewer ask themselves questions before marriage that will flesh out the truth of where they are in their lives and if they are truly ready to make the kind of commitment that marriage requires. This book is significant and has powerful preventive principles that if practiced can greatly reduce the incidents of divorce by educating beforehand of the importance of taking your potential mate to court. This book greatly increases the number of successful marriages as it guides couples to make a more suitable choice using a more in-depth tool for measuring compatibility.

The type of life I live with my wife, Atiya, is a purposeful one. The courtship process prepared me for it and challenged me to do something differently to get a different result. If I had, had sexual intercourse with Atiya prior to marriage, I honestly do not believe that I would have married her, not because I was not attracted to her or that I would have "lost" respect for her, but because I would not have appreciated her in the way that I should appreciate such a gift. There is a saying that, "The man who finds a wife finds a treasure, and he receives favor from the Lord."

The manner in which we "dated" called us both to be responsible and accountable. Likewise, and more importantly, it facilitated a higher level of mutual respect, a clearer perspective, and allowed me as a man to recognize the treasure and not just the booty. It re-enforced the commitment that we both made to not settle or compromise and what we soon realized around the six-month mark is that we in fact wanted to be a part of each other's lives and was not willing to walk away. We discovered that we fit.

They say that hindsight is twenty-twenty. Well, after reading the book, I must say that *Purposeful Dating* is effective, powerful, and on point!

Ingram Jones
Relationship Mentor
Ingram & Atiya Enterprises, LLC.

Table of Contents

Introduction 1

The Meaning of Dating and Courtship 15

Discovering and Accepting Your Own Truth 21

Taking the Steps in the Courtship Process 29

Understanding What Helps and Hurts the Process 87

Conclusion 95

Introduction

Everything we do in our lives must have an aim and purpose in order to exponentially benefit from our efforts. That includes the dating process as well. Whether you are looking for a friend or someone to marry, the mindset going into building a relationship is very important to your outcome, as well as the experiences you have along the way. In this message, I want to share some information that will offer a strategy to help you find that missing link, your "soul-mate," or the love of your life.

First let me say this. If you are looking for a "strictly friendship" relationship with the opposite gender, then your mindset will be very different than if you were looking for a love connection. It is possible for two people of the opposite gender to be only friends. However, usually these sorts of relationships lead to deeper attachments and patterns of interacting that ultimately open the door for love to organically grow. Nature is a powerful phenomenon and no matter how un-attracted you are to a person, if you spend regular time with that person and have consistent deep and meaningful communication, attraction and attachments will occur naturally. This is nature.

Nature refers to the "restorative powers of the body, bodily processes; powers of growth." In its root it means the character, essence or principle of life. Things come to birth naturally and there are behavior patterns that will give rise or birth to certain results. I say this to say that some of the best and most fulfilling intimate relationships start out as "friendships." Therefore, when referring to opposite gender friendships, in most cases, there is no such thing as "just friends."

Often for one or both people in these "strictly friendship" relationships what usually happens as a result of establishing patterns of behaviors and interactions, intimate relationships or the desire for intimate relationships blossom.

If you are not interested in anything other than a friendship, then it is important to avoid planting seeds that will grow naturally under certain types of conditions. It would be wise to understand some things about mating. In the truer sense, men and women can never really be "just friends." The reason for this is nature and the power of nature in the science of mating. While you may know of many cases where men and women say they are just friends and to you they may be only friends because you like many others believe that platonic friendships are ones where there is no sexual intercourse happening in the relationship. However, being just friends or having a platonic relationship means that the relationship is also void of any "feelings" of romantic love or desire and "attraction."

When it comes to the interaction between men and women, authentically being "just friends" is not possible because of the way men and women are wired. At some point in a relationship between opposite genders, whether it is at the onset or somewhere in between; the "strictly friends" relationship becomes complicated by the power of attraction between male and female. This is a natural occurrence and progression and no matter how little attraction there is between the two at the onset, it will inevitably grow between the two over time when there is a pattern of sharing, continual conversations, exchanging of time, sharing of space, and joining for events. This is the power of mating.

This is why arranged marriages work so well, not that I am advocating arranged marriages. Love grows over time when the relationship is undergirded by certain behaviors. In arranged marital situations the ones doing the arranging have already examined the other party therefore the work of courting has already been done. In this case the two people are betrothed. It is just working out the details to "seal the deal." Being "in love" with someone is a euphoric state of mind. In truth, it is a state of mania. Mania is "mental derangement characterized by excitement and delusion." What people often refer to as being in love with another is simply an acknowledgement of the power of attraction they have for that person that goes beyond a superficial attractive energetic pull. Being in love with a person and loving a person intimately are two very different states and conditions of mind.

Instinctively - physiologically speaking, opposite genders have an innate need to procreate, whether they consciously choose it or not; and this instinctive and underlying biological process automatically kicks in at some point when men and women interface. The love and protection factor comes as a result of behaviors being repeated and patterns of interactions being established. This is why love is what you do! Love grows through a demonstration over time. So in essence to be "in love" with someone is to be in the active process of demonstrating that which helps love to grow and flourish. Courtship opens the way for this to happen naturally, likewise so does "friendship" across genders.

Men and women are not just friends of each other. If you believe that then you do not understand the science of mating nor of nature. The "we are just only friends" scenario might be true for one person in the relationship; but rarely if at all is it true overall. When one person in the "friendship" has feelings for another beyond platonic feelings, the relationship ceases to be a "strictly friendship" relationship and this is usually the case in most relationships involving the male/female dynamic. The classification into the "friend zone" or the "strictly friends" boundary, causes people to suppress their true feelings keeping their more than platonic feelings a secret. Often, this is due to the inappropriate "friend" connections or attachment to people who are otherwise engaged in separate intimate relationships or marriages. Because of the necessity to define or explain their relationship with an opposite gender friend to their mate, there is a denial that happens from one or both parties. Two people know when there is an attraction, whether spoken or not, they intuitively know because of receptors or neurotransmitters. No amount of suppression or lying covers over the fact that the relationship is more than a platonic one.

Some people may have a problem with what I am saying. However, if you honestly examine your own emotional state with your so-called opposite gender friends, or have some really serious and deep discussions centered on the nature of your friendship with your opposite gender friend, you will know that what I say is true. Usually at least one person is attracted to the other, although secretly. This takes it out of the friend zone, the platonic zone, or the "we are just friends" zone.

Can men and women be just friends? Not usually. There may be some cases, but in these friendship dynamics, those who are honestly "just friends" have a relationship where there is a very distinctive space between the two. Bona-fide friendships of the opposite gender do not relate like two women who are friends or two men who are friends. There is a clear separation and they do not "hang out." They don't establish patterns of interaction such as going to the movies, out to dinner together, coupling for events, talking on the phone or on chat, Skype or the like. They keep a "safe" distance. Conversations are not regular at all. They are genuinely friends, meaning they genuinely love each other, but not intimately. Yet, this is rare. The only reason two people of opposite gender are able to remain "just friends" is because there is space and lack of bonding so as to prevent the relationship from growing to an intimate level. Yet again, if the feelings or desire to take it to another level is there, it is not platonic. So in truth, really, can men and women normally be just friends? I would say no.

Creating patterns of relating and interacting is a fast track to taking the relationship out of the "friend zone" when you understand the science of mating. Because men and women in truth are not naturally able to be "just friends," again, if you are not interested in organically growing a relationship, then it is important to avoid planting seeds that will grow naturally under certain types of conditions. The same is true with people who "work" together as well.

Does this mean that when you are in a serious relationship or married that you do not communicate or interface with the opposite gender? No, what this means is that you use your mate as a buffer for the exchange in all possible cases and when not possible, you keep the exchange strictly to the point and break it off without extending it. Some people are challenged by this out of not wanting to offend the other person. This is not a case of offending the other person but a case of using wisdom and being strong to maintain loyalty to the one in which you are committed to.

Like I mentioned at the onset, everything we do in our lives must have an aim and purpose in order to exponentially benefit from our efforts. That includes the dating process as well. Your aim and purpose is your intention or what you desire from your efforts. It is what you intend to gain, your goal or target. Most people know exactly what they are aiming for; but some are not honest about their reasons to themselves or others. You know why you do what you do. So be clear and honest about it!

When you are entering into the dating arena, "What is your aim?"
"What are you honestly wanting or hoping to gain by what you are doing?"
"What do you want the end result to be?"

If your aim and purpose is to find your missing link, otherwise that special person for your "happily ever after," let me share with you the power of courtship. This process is for those who are ready and serious about committing to one person and who are willing to go out there and find their Mr. or Mrs. Right using a proven strategy that works.

Chapter 1

The Meaning of Dating and Courtship

To date is to set an appointment for a liaison. The reason for the liaison is for two people to genuinely get to know one another. Dating stems back as far as the mating process itself. It's a method used to help people better sift through potential life partners to find the one who is compatible. A liaison, in its root, means to bind together. The aim and purpose of scheduling dates in its true sense of form has always been a method used to determine a person's suitability as a life partner for marriage. Scheduling dates has always been a part of what is called and referred to as "courting" or the courting process. Understand though that just because you schedule a date with someone, does not mean you are in courtship with them.

Courting is the process by which two people date with the INTENTIONS (aim or purpose) of determining the suitability for marriage. Today, people date for socialization, recreation, or to find a mate. However, in order to find the love of your life or that special person, the process of courting becomes a very powerful method to you sifting through the quantity to get to the quality of what you are looking for. Finding and re-connecting to your "Soul-mate" or "second self" is what this dating and marriage thing is about.

Courtship is a process that is scientifically and supernaturally designed to help you get it right the first time. When your intentions include other than what the process is designed to do – aim for marriage, many headaches and heartaches are the result. When the intentions are true, whether or not you have found your match, the outcome will reflect the good intentions. Dates are the liaisons used to get to the information to determine if the person is the one to move things forward and begin courting. So the process would move from having many one-time dates with several different people to having many dates with one person.

Chapter 2

Discovering and Accepting Your Own Truth

Discovering and accepting your own truth is done prior to making a connection with someone else. To prepare for marriage and connect with the one person who is compatible to you, it is important to know who you are and accept the beautiful gift that you are. There is a person who is right for you and who can actually be a part of "completing" you. Let me help you to put that in context. When two people are compatible they fit together. They are "capable of being used together without special modification or adaptation." They complement one another, which mean they complete and fill up each other. They "feel" one another in a supernatural way and are able to co-exist harmoniously because of the natural "pity" innate in them for the other person.

Pity is loyalty, sense of duty, mercy, compassion, care, tenderness.

You can be attracted to many people and feel a sense of chemistry. However, there is one person who when you are with them or around them there is a spark that goes far beyond just an attraction.

Now at the start of many relationships you may see characteristics of pity. However for two people who are truly compatible this "feeling" toward one another does not diminish, it continues to grow over time. It grows from simple attraction to a spark that lasts and turns into a flame that is fanned.

People, who are compatible, experience blissful states. They do not fall in and out of love with one another. Yes they have disagreements, yes they argue and fight, and yes they have ups and downs. However, a profound love remains at the root and foundation because in them is a supernatural connection that goes far beyond a physical connection. They both have the characteristics and innate "it" factor that fills the space for each other. So when a person says he or she completes me, they are saying, "This person is truly my 'twin,' my 'soulmate,' my 'second-self,' my best friend." That is exactly what the process of courtship is designed to do – help you sift through all the wrong identities to discover the real person who you are meant to connect with. That missing link is the missing part of you.

If you are looking for a specific earring, shoe, tie, or necklace, once you look in a particular place and you do not find it, you don't stick around just because. No! You leave that store or place and continue looking. So why do many people continue to date or bind with people that they know good and well is not the one they want to be with in the long-run? This is something to ask yourself and to keep in mind in your quest to find your husband or wife.

There is a science to mating. Therefore, when you are searching for your counterpart or that missing part of yourself, it makes sense that you would have to know a little something about yourself. Otherwise, how would you even know if you have found the "right" person? To begin the journey of self-discovery please see my book entitled, *From Ordinary to Extraordinary,* 2nd edition, which includes an interactive workbook designed to help you discover your own truth in preparation for a better marriage and life overall.

Some of the questions outlined in the book are:

- Who are you?
- What are four (4) things that are very important to you in life?
- What is your life mission?
- What are your personal, professional, and spiritual goals?

- What are some things you would like to accomplish in your lifetime?
- What are your greatest challenges?
- What are your stressors?
- What actions do you take to minimize stressors?
- What areas in your life would you like to change?
- What do you like to do for fun and enjoyment?

The above are only the tip of the iceberg of questions outlined in the book, *From Ordinary to Extraordinary*. This book is a great tool as you commit and prepare for the process of courting in the context as outlined here because it is strategically designed to guide you through a self-discovery process to finding your truth. Finding your truth is a necessary component to finding your missing link.

Chapter 3

Taking the Steps in the Courtship Process

Step 1 – Scoping the Possibilities (The Search/Prowl)

Most people who are single are on the prowl. It is a natural occurrence. Unfortunately some married people still scope out possibilities too. However, that is another matter altogether. To prowl or scope is to keenly examine or "check out" opportunities for the purpose of pursuing with an end result to capture the intended "prey." In this context, prey meaning the intended target – guy or girl.

Scoping/Prowling is not gender specific. Both men and women scope out possibilities and go on the prowl. Women tend to be more subtly skilled at prowling than men because of an innate sense that comes along with their gender. Women tend to use mating calls (body language, eye contact, and other gestures) sending signals to men that they are available and interested. Men will perceive the opening mostly unconsciously and thus begin pursuing the female. In some cases, especially in today's society, though, it is not uncommon for women to pursue men.

Regardless as to who pursues who, in the mating process both men and women send signals to one another which often starts as non-verbal communication. As a result of these non-verbal clues, the "cat and mouse" game commences. The whole process is actually quite exhilarating for both men and women. Men love the chase and women love being chased. Sparks fly and depending on the skill of one's chase or the other's coyness, it will either lead to many exciting exchanges or fizzle as fast as it starts.

As you begin to search for your missing link, it is a key factor to search with a purpose. No matter how fun the chase may be or how much joy you are having tantalizing your suitor, remember that there is a specific aim for why you are doing what you're doing. The real purpose and intent must always be the focal point of your activity – to find a life-long mate.

So now, the process begins with the search of your other part. No one is whole until connecting to their other part. As a single person, God steps in and fills that void when the intentions are right. You are guided to the one that is for you through this process. However, you must ask yourself some heartfelt questions and be totally honest with yourself in the process.

Some questions you may want to consider and ask yourself are:

- What am I looking for in a life partner?

- Does the person I am pursuing or scoping out have what I want and need in my life?

- Does the person that I am engaging in this process share my vision and mission in life?

- Am I physically attracted to this person?

- How does this person complement me and my life at the moment and how will they complement me in the future?

- Am I really ready to settle down and commit for life?

- Do I have any unresolved issues that would hinder my relationship with this person that I am pursuing?

- Am I ready to be vulnerable to another person and open myself up to sharing intimate space with another person?

- Is there room in my life for another person at the moment?

- Am I ready to re-prioritize all of my other relationships (family, friends, co-workers…) to make this one a priority?

There are many more questions you can ask yourself. However the number one question to answer completely and truthfully is, "Are you ready to settle down to a good choice?"

Settling down to a good choice does not mean to settle for less than what you want and deserve. What I am saying is to search for and find exactly what you are needing and wanting in your life, but then once you have found the one that suits you and the one who you have determined is your "missing link," then make the necessary decision to stop looking and do the right thing. There is some truth to the old adage, "A fox that chases two rabbits don't eat."

Being on the prowl or scoping possibilities is all about searching for your marital partner – that one person to share your life with. Yes, in many cases, in order to make a clear determination as to whether or not you have found that missing part of yourself, you may have to meet, talk to and date several people prior to getting into more serious exchanges.

Yet, your aim and purpose for doing so is to find the one person that is the most compatible with you.

The first step – Scoping the Possibilities requires you to have a clear understanding of what it is you are looking for, otherwise your search is aimless. When searching for a missing person, usually there is a picture of what the person looks like. The same is true here. Know exactly what you are looking for before going on the prowl. If not, you really just end up "playing the field." Playing the field is dating or having sex with more than one person without the intentions of marrying. When a person who is seriously engaging in the process of purposeful dating, they don't' play the field; they search for that one person to spend their life with and every exchange is with the intentions of exploring and accessing information for the possibility of sharing their life with that person.

Step 2 - Making the Connection
(The Introduction)

During the search you will most likely see someone who catches your attention. Perhaps there is already someone you've spotted that you want to meet formally. In moving the process along, your next step once you scope out a potential partner would be to make the connection. In this case, you initiate an introduction or someone initiates it on your behalf such as a family member, mutual friend, co-worker, or church member. Nonetheless, there is some sort of introduction.

Once a connection is made, you may exchange contact information after brief interactions or it may be a scenario where there is a group of people socializing together. The introduction regardless of the situation is a time to get acquainted with the person and to see if there is mutual attraction or interest. Normally this is the time to just observe and not necessarily, "go in for the kill." When a person goes in for the kill, they lay all of their cards on the table. The introduction step is not the time to do this. Although sometimes when an introduction is made, extended conversations may take place because of the situation at hand. In some cases, people may meet through mutual associations or during certain events and end up spending hours together. It is not uncommon under these conditions to have more in-depth conversations with a person you just meet.

There have been times when two people actually make very strong bonds at first meetings when the situation lends itself to spending time together in close proximity for an extended period of time. Some might even characterize these bonds as "love at first sight."

Then there are times when you scope a person out and when you finally meet them face-to-face you find out that there is not a mutual attraction and you determine that you are not interested at all.

So be it. Throw the fish back into the water. You are not under any obligation to move the relationship forward. Therefore, be sure not to lead the person on or give them the impression that there is an interest when there's not.

While scoping and during the introduction, men and women will often flirt with one another. The flirtations may be overt or subtle. This is very natural. There is nothing vulgar about it. However, keep in mind some flirting can be considered crossing the line or inappropriate, depending on the character of the person you are interacting with. Your intentions will guide you. When you remember that you are not looking for a one night stand, but rather a life partner, your manner of behaving will more than likely be much more respectful and considerate.

Flirting is to behave in a manner inclining toward love, but in the absence of an emotional commitment. The point of the flirt is to get the attention of the one with whom you are flirting to communicate interest or notice so that possibly an emotional attachment can ultimately take place. Some silly people will flirt when it's not appropriate. For example, flirting with someone else's mate is off limits for a person who is dating with a purpose; not that it is appropriate any other time. If that man or woman is not your espoused, marriage partner, or one who is free to engage in a long-term relationship, then flirting is foolish. It stirs up trouble. Playing with affairs of the heart is a dangerous game.

Likewise, why flirt when you don't intend to take it further? To do so is just playing immature games and teasing people. Do you really want to tug at people's heart strings? Not if you are a respectable person you don't. Some silly women will flirt with men who are taken just to see if they can pull his attention away from his wife or intended. Some men do the same. Again, this is a dangerous game, and the truth is if you behave dishonorably in this manner, ultimately you are the one who gets hurt. If you want a wife or a husband, it's time to put the childish games aside, and get real about it.

Step 3 – Opening the Dialogue (The Conversation)

Once you get to the conversation, it is only fair to inform the person of your true intentions. This is especially important for men. However, this is not gender specific because it is important that both men and women place their true intentions on the table. The conversation stage often happens on the phone or on a date. There are many layers to the conversation. It happens sort of like peeling an onion. In other words, information is shared gradually; and sometimes information may make you tear up. It can be that deep.

With an onion, there are layers. Likewise in a first conversation you would not share really personal, private, or extremely sensitive information. On a first or second date, you may discuss general information about how you grew up or things that impacted you greatly in your life. However, by the time the conversation reaches the courtship stage, you'll find yourself being much more open and transparent.

When you have that first or second conversation, if you are a man, the way you state your intentions may be somewhat different than how a woman would state what she is looking for. If you are a man, you might say something like, "I have to be totally honest; I do not date just to be dating. My goal is to find the person that I can spend the rest of my life with."

If the person you are speaking with is one that you would like to continue exploring possibilities with, ask them where they are in terms of marriage or a serious relationship that will ultimately lead toward marriage. Ask them if they are in a place in their life where they are ready to settle down. When you do this, it opens up the dialogue for deeper and more directed conversations in this "dating game." Let the person know where you are in terms of what you hope to gain. This helps you to make your intentions very clear. I would also like to add that I use "dating game" loosely because love in truth is not a game and when games are played with the affairs of the heart, everyone loses.

If you are on a date with a woman that you are not interested in exploring the possibilities with, it is better to cut the interactions off fairly quickly. Sometimes you may have to gently share with her that you do not see yourself with her at the end of this journey and that because you do not want to lead her on, you think it best to continue the journey of finding your wife. This may be a hard thing to do, but it saves a lot of headaches and heartaches in the long-run. It's a mature thing to do. If you are on a date, you both can agree to continue the date cordially and wish each other the best. To some people that might sound cold, but it is not.

What is cold is to lead a person on and lead them to believe that you are interested when you are not, all because you don't have the courage to face the situation honestly.

Also, let me say this to you men reading this book. It's wise not to open up the opportunity to be friends in order to keep the conversations going or to avoid, "hurting her feelings." Remember that you are on a mission and maintaining opposite gender close nit friendships only complicates matters. In heterosexual situations, it's possible for men and women to be "just friends." At some point and time in the friendship, as stated before, one or both parties begin to develop intimate feelings. If the woman is not the one you want to move things further with, then don't move things further with her. It's as simple as that.

Women get upset, not because men are not interested in them, but rather because some men lead them on knowing full well that they are not interested. Some men will talk sweet, will say things that give the impression that it is more to it than it really is, and later down the road after perhaps having had a few "rolls in the hay" or "naps in the sack," he decides that he really wasn't interested in anything more than having a good time. This is what gets women upset.

Now, if you are a woman wanting to state your intentions, in the first conversation or when the opportunity arises you could say something like, "I have decided to keep myself for my husband. I am serious about wanting to get married and I am not looking for a relationship void of having the potential to move to a life-long and exclusive commitment. I will not allow myself to get connected or attached to someone who is not serious about making that commitment or who is not in the place in their life where they are ready to settle down to a good choice." The woman can then say something like this. "I do not believe in the '90-rule,' for me the rule is to keep the cookie in the cookie jar until marriage." Then she can give the most beautiful smile.

The same applies to women as men in terms of leading someone on that you are really not interested in moving forward with. Avoid making men think that they have a chance when you know you are not interested in them. However, remember to let him down easy. If you are interested, ask him where he is in his life and if he is looking for a long-term commitment. Ask him very directly, is he looking for a wife, and find out what he is looking for.

Both of you may very well be looking for that long-term relationship. However, it does not mean that you will find it in each other. Therefore it is essential to communicate openly about what you want and what you are looking for. Don't be afraid to want what you want for fear of not finding it. Your twin is out there somewhere and it is up to you to find your missing link. However you have to be honest if you expect to find the one who is compatible to you. Marriage brings out the truth. Therefore if you lie on the front end that lie will quickly become manifest in the marriage dynamic. Always be true to who you are, because what you are looking for is the other part of yourself.

Step 4 – Making the Necessary Observations (The Date)

The date itself is a really fun way to get to know someone. It is important to date because it allows two people to observe one another to see how they connect and interact with each other. Dates can range from having dinner and going to a movie or going hiking, skiing or walking in the park. They can be as simple or extravagant as you choose.

One thing to keep in mind as you organize your dates is to set very real and clear expectations. If you really cannot afford a particular date, why do it? How you start out something is going to be what is expected. If you do something extravagant and it is not normally the way you would do things, be clear to the other person and let them know that this is something special and not the norm for you. While you may strive to be able to do a thing more often or consistently, if it is not true for you at the moment, make that clear. You want to be as open and honest as possible.

The other thing about dates is this: Be clear on who you expect to pay and deal head on with your belief systems around this topic. Some women are very traditional and expect men to court them and pay for everything. Some women believe that it should be shared. Determine what your belief systems are and be honest about them.

Every date is an opportunity to engage in very meaningful conversation. As communication and conversations become more in-depth, it is important to cover all of the foundational aspects of a person such as:

- Has a person been married before?

- Does the person have any children? How many?

- What are the ages?

- Do you want children? More children?

- If married before, why divorced? Who left who? Was it a mutual decision?

- When was the last relationship? What were the circumstances surrounding the break-up?

- What is your educational background?

- What is your family structure? Siblings?

- How did you grow up? Where did you grown up? What was the environment like in which you grew up?

- What is your life mission? Your dreams? Your goals?

- What is your full name? What other names have you used? What names were you called by when growing up?

- How is your relationship with your father? Your mother?
- What is your family lineage?
- What are your likes? Dislikes? Pet peeves?
- What is your style of leadership? Relating?
- What is your style of discipline? Of rewarding?
- What do you do for fun?
- What is your health situation?

There are so many questions a person can ask, going deeper as the occasion calls for it. The above are only a few areas to observe and explore. Two people may be very attracted to one another, but are they compatible? For example, you may have an overweight person and an athlete that meet up. There might be some mutual attraction; but if the person who is overweight is not striving to lose weight, yet the athlete loves to hike and participate in other physical and/or sporty activities, this may not be a compatible situation, especially if the athlete is looking for a mate who is willing and/or able to participate in these activities. It is important to explore as much as possible throughout the dating process, no matter how difficult of a feat it might appear to be.

It does not take long to determine whether or not you want to continue getting to know a person or if he/she is compatible with you. In the first, second or third date, it is pretty easy to ascertain that information. The problem is, people often engage in recreational dating and have no aim or purpose, nor reason or rhyme or "method to their madness." As a result, they wander aimlessly in the process and carry a lot of baggage that they should have otherwise dropped off along the way.

Something to keep in mind with respect to purposeful dating...Keep dates in the public domain. Avoid organizing dates that would temp you or the other person sexually. If you would like to organize a date to take place at a less public venue, then be sure to invite another couple or other people along. While they may not have to be up under the two of you, they can serve as a barrier to prevent certain activities from taking place or behaviors that lead to sexual activities.

Nature is a strong force and when two people are together given the right circumstances, things can happen and they often do. There are many babies that were born as a result of one-night stands. If one of your aims is to not engage in certain types of exchanges, then don't place yourself in certain environments that would otherwise lend itself to such things. Avoid going in a direction that you do not want or intend to go in. This is a conscious decision that two people make, and it takes maturity to do so.

Purposeful dating is about getting to know one another for the purpose of marriage and doing so without having pre-marital sex, which clouds a person's judgment during discovery. Again, engaging in sexual intercourse prior to marriage impedes the examination process. Establishing emotional bonds designed for the marriage relationship is definitely a matter that will complicate things. So why create bonds or establish cords with someone who you have no intentions of being with? The whole idea behind sexual expression with your mate is to form strong, unbreakable bonds and attachments. To have sex with someone that you do not want to be with is an oxymoron – more simply put, it's "pointedly foolish."

If you need to "get your rocks off," take a cold shower or something, but keep your candy bar in its wrapper and the cookie in the cookie jar! If you are used to having sex all the time and then decide to purposefully date, it may be a challenge but eventually you will find many ways to control your urges. Diet is one way, but that's another book.

Utilize the dates to have fun and explore the possibilities. This is an exciting time and although it is a serious matter it can actually unfold through some really exciting activities. Express your true self because if you don't the very thing about you that you keep hidden may be the very thing that the other person find irresistibly attractive and the very sign to let the other person know that perhaps you are the one for them. Physical intimacy does not have to be part of the equation to have fun. There is nothing in the "dating rule book" that says you must kiss on dates. I am not telling you not to nor am I telling you to kiss. I am saying to be you, and be mindful not to lead a person on.

Purposeful dating is responsible dating. The activities you set up to explore possibilities ultimately are to make a determination as to whether or not you want to take the relationship to the next level - the next level being entering into a formalized courtship situation. It is true, you may have to "kiss a few frogs" before finding the right one. It may take dating a few different people before you actually make the right connection or find the one you have been looking for. Don't be afraid to get in there; just remember to keep it clean!

Step 5 - Taking a Closer Look and Examination – (The Courtship/Pre-Engagement)

Entering into a formalized courtship takes the relationship to a much more serious level. However, it is the natural progression the relationship takes when you determine that you have found what you have been looking for. The formalized courtship or pre-engagement step is where both people get down to the nitty-gritty of the examination process, asking the really tough questions and discussing the really serious stuff. Not that you don't discuss important things before now, it is the time to "bare all."

The conversations become much more intimate, personal, and sensitive. Dates continue to take place, but they become more focused on exploring marital situations. For example, in the pre-engagement step, the dating process may include you cooking for your court or preparing meals together. It may include meeting each other's families and having serious discussions with family members, pastors or other spiritual influences. It may also include some preliminary discussions with marital counselors or spiritual advisors to assist in the examination process, and to help you explore issues that you otherwise would not have thought of such as blended family scenarios, holiday considerations, religion, education, finances.

The courtship or "*pre-engagement*" is when dating definitely becomes exclusive and the relationship is bound in advance by an informal promise. Although during conversations, there have been many subjects explored and discussed. Herein is where the serious examination and exploration takes place. No question is off-limits. Some things you may want to explore and examine in great detail may include:

Spiritual Life:

- Theological beliefs
- Spiritual house attendance
- Prayer life/Scriptural study habits
- Spiritual strengths/weaknesses
- Spiritual gifts/witnessing
- Family spiritual belief systems

Interpersonal Relationships:

- Relationship with mother and father
- Relationship with siblings
- Relationship with grandparents
- Relationship with extended family
- Relationship with friends
- Relationship and interaction with peers
- Relationship with co-workers
- Relationship to government/civil servants

- Relationship with children

Marital Roles/Family structure:

- Attitudes toward men/women
- Attitudes toward children
- Number of children wanted
- Ideas of the role of husband/wife
- How conflict is handled
- Previous relationships/marriages
- How to spend holidays
- Level of affection
- Position on corporal punishment/manner of discipline
- Position on child-rearing
- Ability to accept personal responsibility and be accountable
- Work/home balance

- Level of transparency, openness, communication style

- Ability to easily forgive

Habits:

- Cleanliness and hygiene

- Manners and etiquette

- Diet and eating habits

- Physical fitness or wellness/well-being

- Intake of water

- Appearance

- Spending habits

- Sleeping patterns, positions, side of bed

- Pet peeves, annoying habits

- Work ethic

- Household contributions

- Attitude toward things, material possessions

Morality/Character:

- Life values
- Position on manner of dress
- Alcohol, tobacco or drug use
- Fidelity/infidelity issues
- Behavior patterns toward keeping word
- Pornography issues, attitude on pornography
- Profanity or offensive language
- Honesty and trustworthiness
- Charitable spirit
- Supportive nature
- Kindness, gratefulness, just
- Respectful, fair, caring, cares for community
- Abuse issues –physical, mental, emotional, sexual

Sexuality:

- Sexual history
- Sexually transmitted diseases (STD's)
- Sexual responsibility
- Healthy behaviors sexually
- Faithfulness/promiscuity
- Attitude toward sex
- Likes and dislikes
- Abuse issues
- Ability to communicate sexual needs and wants
- Views on birth control/abortion

Influences:

- Attitude toward pets
- Leadership ability – leader or follower
- Primary influences in life

- Interests, talents/gifts, hobbies
- Friendships/family
- Coachable or teachable spirit
- Ability to balance and keep things in perspective
- Television, media, sports, other activities
- Work/co-workers/colleagues

Miscellaneous:

- Education
- Allergies
- Health conditions
- Career and career aspirations
- Life's mission
- Purpose in life
- Strengths/weaknesses
- View on pets – inside/outside, sleep with, freedom to roam, like/don't like

- Tendencies toward cultural intolerance, racism, prejudice

- Sports and other physical activities

- Spare time activities

- Temptations, weaknesses

Sample questions:

1). Is the relationship with parents an honoring and obedient one?

2). Is he/she a leader or influencer among peers?

3). What is his/her sleep pattern like?

4). Does he/she tend toward workaholic or other extreme behaviors?

5). Is he/she orderly and organized?

6). Is he/she fiscally responsible? Is there a problem with finances?

7). In making decision, what role does God or God's word factor in?

8). What is his attitude toward women? Her

attitude toward men?

9). Is there any alcohol, drugs, or tobacco use or has there been in the past?

10. What is his/her attitude toward pets?

11. Has he/she ever hit a man/woman?

12. Has he/she ever been arrested? For what?

13. Has he/she ever been unfaithful or disloyal in a relationship?

14. What is the view on sacred days or holy days?

15. What is his/her life purpose and life mission?

16. What is a typical day like from waking up to going to bed?

17. What is the view of food, eating habits, do's and don'ts?

18. Is he/she a person of his/her word? Does he/she keep their word when they give it?

19. How many children does he/she want?

20. Are there any physical or mental disabilities?

Keep in mind, some of the above questions might have already been answered and information ascertained. However, if they haven't you definitely want to take the conversations to a deeper level to be able to gather the information needed and desired. Examine the person's character; get character references. Ask family member and friends tough questions. The above are not all-inclusive. They only serve as a guide to help you ask the tough questions and to do your due diligence in learning as much as possible about the person you have an arrangement with.

Some people may initially avoid such in-depth, exploratory or invasive line of questioning and probing. However, it is very important to cover all bases and ask the necessary questions. Likewise it is necessary to observe the person to see if their actions are congruent and consistent with their words.

This pre-engagement step is about making an advance promise prior to the actual promise of marriage and entering into the formalized engagement process. You can understand it perhaps a little better from the perspective or in the context of a company giving a potential employee an offer of employment based on the contingency that everything checks out and the background check and physical/health check comes back acceptable. It is a very similar concept except that in this case the job or role is that of husband or wife; and that in truth is one of the most important jobs or roles a person can have.

When you enter into courtship with a person, the main objective is to examine and analyze the situation very carefully to confirm that this is in fact the missing part of yourself. The actual courtship/pre-engagement step should take no more than six months. This is not something to play around with. This is why it is important to make sure you are ready for marriage.

Conducting an examination is crucial. Yet, even more important is to abstain from sexual intercourse. Having sex before marriage impedes the process as it brings in certain emotions that are designed to come in to play after marriage and after the examination. Your emotions should not be the guiding factor for making decisions, especially one as important as choosing a life partner. Be sober in your process of looking for a mate, and remain celibate. During the process, celibacy helps tremendously in opening the way for you to see more clearly. Many people don't understand the importance of this aspect of courting, but I guarantee that it elevates the nature and character of the process. Further, it eliminates the so-called "mistakes" from happening. Of course no child conceived is a mistake regardless of the circumstances of how the pregnancy came about.

Step 6 – Formalizing the Promise (The Engagement)

After you have taken a closer look and conducted the necessary examination, and after you believe that all due diligence has been done – you've asked all the questions that needed to be asked and ascertained all the information that you could possibly learn about your court to be sure that he/she is in fact the one that you have been looking for, then it is time for the next step. It is time to get engaged!

The Engagement is the part of the process where you formally ask the person to marry you, particularly if you are a man who proactively set out on this journey. If you are a woman who has taken the step to purposefully date and take this course of finding true love, then it is likely that your court will ask you as he would be well aware of the process too, because you would have introduced it to him. At some point, he would have become very much a part of the process. If you are a woman, it is even more important that you make your position known at the onset. Your behavior will help whatever man you connect with understand how serious you are in building a lasting relationship at the onset, and that any dating past a certain point will either result in marriage or the end of the process as you are looking for that ultimate commitment.

Traditionally speaking, men are the ones who usually lead the process in that the majority of women still wait on men to propose. However, this is not necessarily true in all cases. There are some women who do propose to men. Yet, more men propose to women, and if you are a woman who has taken the step to engage in the journey of purposeful dating, and you hold the position that a man should propose to you, then it is especially important for you to embark upon this whole process with sincerity, consistency, and openness. You want to know for sure that your potential mate is ready for marriage and has no bones about asking you to marry him if you both decide that "this is the one." However rest assured that these discussions would have naturally occurred during the many conversations that took place prior to the Courtship/Pre engagement.

With that being said, the formal engagement process begins with a proposal of marriage. Once a proposal of marriage is made and accepted, then the next thing to do is plan for the actual date of the wedding ceremony. Earlier we discussed that the Courtship/Pre-engagement was like a contingent job offer. Well, the engagement or formalized promise can be considered as the formal job offer. After a company has conducted the final interviews, and the test results and medical exams have all come back favorable, they will provide a formal job offer.

When there is a formal job offer, there is a start date, salary agreement, and the department specified. Once the employee starts, training commences for the new role. This is very similar. In the process of purposeful dating, the engagement is brief. It is only long enough to allow the couple to prepare for the marriage ceremony. A date is set at the onset, and the only time factor is the time it takes to plan the ceremony depending on how large or small you and your mate agree for it to be.

In the purposeful dating process, engagements may last from one to six months, depending on the type of ceremony and everything that is involved in its planning. On rare occasions it may take a little longer, but normally in this process people have the wedding ceremony within six months of the proposal.

Along the way, conversations usually take place where part of the planning perhaps may have already been done. So the couple may know the details of where they would want to get married, where they would live, who would conduct the ceremony, and all of the other details that are usually organized during the planning stages. This is why having meaningful conversations are very important at every stage of the process because it cuts through the bureaucracy of the matter.

Many people drag the process out usually out of fear. However, when you have made a firm decision on the purpose of why you are dating, and you are definitely ready for the long-term commitment, then you won't waste time on being indecisive or dragging the process out. A person who is truly operating in purpose and have an aim for what they do, they are diligent about crossing all "T's" and dotting all "I's." They take this thing seriously and they do not play games with it. They are truly on a mission, and their behavior will demonstrate their level of seriousness. If you are serious about the process, your actions will show it. Men and women who truly set out to find, "the one," usually finds them. It is a matter of making a decision that this is what you want and being ready to commit.

During the engagement, some of the questions or considerations you might want to explore and cover include:

- Announcements
- The date of the wedding ceremony
- The place of the wedding ceremony (city, state, country…)
- The venue where ceremony will take place
- The type of wedding ceremony (church, beach, park, back yard…)
- Size of wedding ceremony
- Budget for the ceremony (based on all contributions)
- How many guests will be in attendance?
- Who are the guests that will be invited?
- Who will the wedding party include?
- Who will perform the ceremony? (Pastor, priest, reverend…)

- Will there be an after the wedding celebration such as a reception?
- Who will be the photographers, caterers, florists?
- Will there be entertainment?
- What will you wear?
- What will the wedding party wear?
- Will guests be traveling from out of town; do you need to block hotel rooms for guests?
- Guest lists
- Gift registry
- Will there be a honeymoon?
- Invitations and save the date cards
- Thank you cards
- Transportation to and from ceremony and after ceremony celebration
- Rehearsals, before wedding dinners, or other activities

- Rings
- Necessary marriage licenses
- People to help on wedding day or prior to
- ceremony

These are just some of the things to cover when planning the wedding ceremony. Perhaps you rather have something small with just you and your intended and the necessary witnesses. It is up to you. However, what's important is to decide, set the date, and follow-through.

You are bound to have disagreements when discussing many of the above topics. Work through them and remember little disputes and disagreements should not be deal-breakers. When having the discussions you will discover ways to work together to come to an agreement. After all, once the wedding ceremony is completed, married life is about synergizing and working together to make both of your dreams a reality. That is not necessarily an easy task. However, if you respect and honor one another, and move from a single mindset to a married/team mindset, things will flow much smoother.

Step 7 – Making the Commitment
(The Wedding Ceremony)

Making the commitment – The Wedding Ceremony is much more than just a "piece of paper" as some people may say. Usually people throw that up as a defense for their unwillingness or fear of making the commitment or by those who have made the decision to "shack" or live together but not marry. People who say, "A piece of paper does not marry us" truly do not fully understand the depth of this thing. It is not about the "piece of paper" at all.

The wedding ceremony is about sealing the formal promise that was made in private and about the couple "locking-in" their word by following the private promise with a public declaration, which is a necessary step to solidifying a promise or making it whole. During the wedding ceremony, the couple's union is actually being made sacred and consecrated. Thus, the term "wedlock" is ascribed to the condition of marriage because at this point the couple is being "locked-in" to a sacred covenant and agreement to give themselves over to a way of life in devotion and trust to one another.

If the wedding ceremony does not take place, the promise is not made whole. The wedding ceremony, regardless if it takes place with just you, the reverend and two witnesses or in the presence of hundreds of guests at a mega spiritual house or cathedral, it is significant because it is a sacred process where a declaration is made openly as a testament of you and your mate's love for one another and your willingness to back that love with your life.

The "piece of paper" making reference to the marriage license itself has no more significance to the wedding ceremony than does booking a venue or having a place to hold the ceremony. It is a matter of detail that must be taken care of, but has no real bearing on the commitment or the promise itself. The marriage license is obtained as a matter of keeping in line with the laws of the land; however the "piece of paper" as one says is not what makes two people married, true. The wedding ceremony is the process by which a union is solemnized or made whole and a covenant partnership entered into.

When a promise is made, there is an "expressed assurance upon which expectations are to be based." To promise is to send forth or make a declaration of what is to come. The wedding ceremony fulfills the formalized promise made when you entered into the engagement step. In other words, you did what you said you would do. That completes that.

Yet, during the wedding ceremony, vows are said in order to lock you and your mate into a covenant or agreement. Vows are solemn promises. A formalized promise like the promise that an engagement represents is the process by which you give shape, meaning, definition or purpose to your relationship and union. The solemn promise that is made during the ceremony is an oath that you and your mate make committing yourself to an act, service, condition, or state of being.

So while the wedding ceremony fulfills one aspect of your word by making clear, revealing, disclosing, and announcing publicly that you have fulfilled your promise of marriage as stated when you became engaged; it also serves as a guarantee. During the ceremony you and your mate give yourselves in sacred trust to one another as surety for the fulfillment of an obligation. That obligation being whatever you stated in the vows.

When two people choose to simply live together, but do not go through the process to consecrate their union, they in essence are not fully committing to the relationship. In other words, they are not completely uniting or entrusting one another. They have not entered into a mutual covenant that is the bedrock of a solid foundation of their union. The covenantal commitment is a higher conviction and purpose. To enter into this type of commitment is like building your house on solid ground. To simply live together is like building your house upon sand.

This process is not to be entered into lightly, nor is mating with another person. Some people are together for years and never have the wedding ceremony. They fall into this category referred to as "common law." Common in its root means shared by all and open. See, the process of having an actual wedding ceremony whether small, private, intimate or large is not about the event or the paper that accompany it, but rather about the declaration, the vow, the covenant.

Common law situations are open, the process of holy matrimony is closed, and it's sealed. It makes a world of difference when you understand that the wedding ceremony is not about getting a piece of paper, but about something far greater and more significant. The reason why courting is so critically important is because you do not want to seal the wrong relationship. Sealing the wrong relationship together is like implanting the wrong organ into a body. You will end up having to re-open the person and remove the incorrect part, otherwise in the marital context known as divorce. The goal is to mate properly. Purposeful dating is a very effective way to manifest the love of your life through the power of courtship.

No matter how many excuses people tend to come up with, no matter what fears people hide behind or limiting belief systems they have, the fact of the matter is that the best relationships grow organically through a process where there is purposeful action. If you want to have the best chances of success in your relationships where there is a built-in respect and openness factor that begins at the onset of the relationship, then courtship is the way to go. In this type of process, the relationship starts out on a higher and purposeful plane; therefore the results are usually more favorable. In anything you do, the intentions you put into it will determine the quality of what you get out of it.

Step 8 – Toiling to Become One
(The Marriage/Re-Connection)

The re-connection process or the marriage is a lifelong journey. It's not always peachy. Yet the rewards are gathered over time, so be encouraged to uphold your vows and work hard to nourish your relationship to keep it in good condition. The number one component to keeping your marriage in tact is to leave and cleave.

Cleaving is to adhere closely, cling to, be glued to, or stick to. It is said "that at the beginning the Creator 'made them male and female, and said, 'For this reason a man will leave his father and mother and be united to his wife, and the two will become one flesh. So they are no longer two, but one flesh. Therefore what God has joined together, let no one separate."

To be one flesh is to become one unit or entity. Prior to marriage, there are two entities or two separate units. After marriage the idea is to become one – a couple. This new entity or unit now becomes the basis for any act, decision, or case that serves as guidance or justification for successive situations. It becomes the precedent of any other relationships past, present or future notwithstanding one's personal relationship with Creator.

When two people decide to marry, they leave the world of singleness, single thinking, single ideology, and single movement to now accept a new way of life emotionally, spiritually, intellectually, financially, and even physically. Both the husband and wife must shift their thinking from "I" to "We."

I have heard a few people say that anything with two heads is a monster in the heat of disagreement. These are people who are still struggling with the "We" concept. The "I" is never placed above the "We" in an authentic Godly and healthy marriage. The head is neither male nor female, rather a synergistic flow of the two. Yin and Yang is a classic example of how there is a natural duality of both energies in one. Where you see Yin, you also see Yang because they each are always present in the other, although perhaps at varying degrees depending on the situation. Yin and Yang balance each other.

Yin and Yang complements each other. They are not opposing forces, but rather interdependent and interacts to form a synergistic whole which is much greater than either part separately. In essence, they form a dynamic system which benefits both forces on a much higher plane of existence. Marriage is designed to do the same.

As a married couple, you will face many challenges. These difficulties will help to strengthen your relationship. Just remember that you are one. Work together. There will be forces that come against your union. Place protective hedges around your marriage. Work together and do not allow your emotions to get the best of you. Stay loyal to your mate.

Chapter 4

Understanding What Helps and Hurts the Process

There are many things that help the process of purposeful dating and there are many things that hurt it. The following is designed to help you be aware of situations and factors that can hinder the process and equip you with information and tools that will help you on your journey to becoming successful.

Things that Help the Process:

Be honest – Be honest with yourself and the other person. Being honest protects the integrity of the entire process. It also lays a foundation filled with honorable ingredients. Fruits that swell from the seeds of honesty produce a prosperous well that runs forth.

Be transparent – Being transparent builds trust and character. It is important to be able to make an informed decision. How would you like it if someone was not honest with you and you made a life-changing decision on what they said to you?

Be courageous to express your truth – Truth is not always easy, particularly when you know it may have the potential to hurt someone's feelings or expose information that may be difficult to bear. It is important that truth is in season. For example, it is not wise to blurt out everything about yourself on the first date. However, it is critical that at some point during discussions at the appropriate times, you disclose information that may have the potential to be deal-breakers.

Date with a purpose – Know why you are doing what you are doing and avoid dating just to be dating. Determine commonalities and lifestyles. It may take a series of dates to make the determination and other times it may take only one or even just a conversation to know that this is the person for you. Does it mean that you jump immediately to the engagement? No! But it does mean you can begin to exclusively explore that particular person to dig deeper.

Examine carefully – Ask the hard questions and have discussions in order to cut through to the heart of the matter at hand. Determine the suitability of a person for marriage and allow them to get to know you. Ask the intimate questions. It may be hard during the process; however, it will most certainly help you develop open lines of communication for the future. People who are able to communicate openly during the process of courting will most likely transfer that behavior over to a marriage as long as they remain open.

Things that Hinders the Process:

Dishonesty – If you are not honest during the process, what will come out of it is the same quality of what you put into it. Lying and expecting to build something of quality is like building a house on sand and telling the other person it is concrete.

Sex - Having sex during the process will most definitely cloud your judgment and is actually putting the cart before the horse. The examination aspect is about getting to the truth of the matter. When you have sex prior to finding the truth, it clouds your judgment. It is important to be sober-minded going into this and making the ultimate decision to marry. Prevent yourself from getting drunk by lust. Wait until the wedding night to share that very special side of yourself with your mate.

Playing the field – If your intentions are not right going into this process, you most likely will not get a positive outcome. Going out on dates with more than one person is very different than dating more than one person at a time. You may have a date one week with a person, another date with a different person next week, and another one with someone else the week after that. However, an example of dating more than one person at a time would be to continuing seeing all three of those people simultaneously. That's not cool!

The goal is to see which one of those three would be the one you would like to explore things a little closer with. If you look deeper and determine that the person is not the one, continue to date other people, but cut things off with that person because you know they are not the one. Once you realize a person is not the one for you, move on and do not continue to attempt to bind the relationship or lead a person on.

Playing enticement, manipulation, or temptation games – Why play games with people's heart? It might be fun for you, but someone always gets hurt. Be real and don't play games with people.

Flirting is one thing, but to tease is another. Stay strong and help the other person remain strong. Avoid placing yourselves in situations that would increase the level of temptation or make it even more difficult to stay abstinent. Also avoid being manipulative or intentionally entice someone as to become weak or make them weak. This is a serious step and decision in life, handle it as such.

Not asking questions or examining carefully – The whole process is designed to get to know the other person and for the other person to get to know you in preparation for marriage. It is important to ask the tough questions and have the difficult conversations. Not asking the tough questions or having those difficult conversations makes it very hard to get to know each other and it makes for a superficial connection.

Not being open – Dating with a purpose helps you to keep both feet on the ground. It is a process that requires complete openness at various levels of interaction. While the process is like peeling an onion and each layer is peeled away at appropriate times when it is comfortable for you and the person you are interacting with, nonetheless, it is important to get through those layers.

Sometimes it is hard to be open, but this process calls for complete openness and not omitting important factors. The decisions made at each junction are made through conversations, examination, exploration, investigation, and research. Do your due diligence to be open, while also minimizing difficulty factors that automatically comes along with purposeful dating.

Conclusion

The world has become extremely small as a result of technology. People are able to work online, go to school online, and also meet and date online. Some people have found extraordinary success with relationships that started from an online connection. One of the powers of online interaction and dating is that it's easier to remove the physical aspect of the relationship and to engage in meaningful conversation to stimulate the relationship. However, it can be very risky because of all of the variables that exist and the masks that people wear. These coverings are very easy to keep on when communicating online. However, by taking conversations to a deeper level and interacting with aim and purpose, you'd be amazed at how intriguing, exciting, and beautiful online interactions are. Yet, at some point it must be brought into the "real" world and out of the virtual one, and that too must be done with care.

Regardless as to the method you meet that special someone, Purposeful Dating is a profound way to manifest the love of your life through the power of courtship. Try it and your life will never be the same.

Thank you. Be blessed. Until next time, keep it real!

THE END

About the Author

ATIYA, founder of The Marriage Tree, has, over the past 20 years, dedicated her life to honing her craft and, indeed, her calling - to empower, build and maximize human potential by affecting profound transformation in people's attitudes, perspectives and behaviors. She has been the catalyst responsible for inspiring countless people worldwide to realize their dreams and achieve joy, success and fulfillment in life.

Now she's bringing all her past experiences, education, and business-development skills from her considerable history as a speaker, author and life coach to focus on her core message: marital harmony ~ extended and profound.

Yes! It is possible to have an enduring relationship that is a positive and rewarding experience for both partners. But like anything of value, it requires fine-tuning and the willingness to learn to navigate the intricacies and subtleties of the changes any marriage encounters during its lifetime. Marriage is organic - it changes, evolves, grows - or like many living things, without proper nurturing, it can deteriorate. But the good news is: it doesn't have to break down. Building a history is a worthwhile, satisfying goal, as well as a tangible legacy for your children.

Atiya is at once an optimist and a pragmatist. She's a firm believer in the reality of a happy and satisfying long term marriage. But she's no Pollyanna, having herself encountered the vagaries of marriages over the past 21 years. She has come through them stronger and happier, gratefully committed, and she can help you to achieve the same result! She'll be the first to tell that what she's going to show you won't be easy, but she's sure of one thing - it will be worth it!

You deserve to live a life filled with mutual inspiration and genuine respect. Atiya has the resources - intellectually and empathetically - to guide you to fruitful solutions that will not only positively-impact your relationship, but, as importantly, will leave you personally empowered.

More Titles By Atiya

From Ordinary to Extraordinary

Hidden Pearls

Petals of a Rose

The Beauty of Being Free

Love is Not a Game

Overcoming the Pain of Losing a Mother

www.ingramcontent.com/pod-product-compliance
Lightning Source LLC
Chambersburg PA
CBHW071714040426
42446CB00011B/2057